HOW TO USE
SEXTANT
FOR BEGINNERS

"A comprehensive and practical step by step navigation guidebook on how to use a sextant even as a complete beginner"

Benjamin L. Hedwig

Benjamin L. Hedwig

How to use a sextant for beginners

How to use a sextant for beginners

© 2023 by Benjamin L. Hedwig

All rights reserved. No part of this publication may be reproduced, stored in a retrieval system, or transmitted, in any form or by any means, electronic, mechanical, photocopying, recording, or otherwise, without the prior permission of the copyright owner, except for brief quotations in critical reviews or articles.

This book is sold subject to the condition that it shall not, by way of trade or otherwise, be lent, resold, hired out, or otherwise circulated without the publisher's prior consent in any form of binding or cover other than that in which it is published and without a similar condition being imposed on the subsequent purchaser.

Benjamin L. Hedwig

How to use a sextant for beginners

Table Of Contents

Introduction 4
Welcome and Introduction to Celestial Navigation 7
    Key Celestial Bodies: 7
    Navigational Tools: 8
    Basic Concepts: 8
    Steps in Celestial Navigation: 9
    Challenges: 9
Importance of Learning Sextant Navigation in the Modern Age 10
Chapter 1 14
The Basics of Celestial Navigation 14
    Understanding Celestial Navigation 14
        Historical Significance and Evolution 15
        Relevance in Modern Navigation 17
    Introduction to Sextants 20
        Anatomy and Components 20
        Types of Sextants and Their Uses 23
    Fundamental Principles 27
        Angle Measurement and Angular Distance 27
        Relationship between Earth, Celestial Bodies, and Observer 31
Chapter 2 35
Nautical Almanacs and Essential Tools 35
    Navigational Almanacs 35

Structure and Content 38
How to Read and Interpret 42
Additional Tools for Celestial Navigation 46
Chapter 3 50
Celestial Bodies and Their Navigation 50
The Sun: Your Primary Celestial Object 50
Taking Sights on the Sun 51
Corrections and Calculations 51
Navigating by the Moon, Planets, and Stars 52
Methods for Taking Sights on Various Celestial Bodies
.... 53
Overcoming Challenges and Pitfalls 56
Special Cases and Techniques 60
Twilight Navigation 63
Stellar Navigation and Fixing Positions at Night 65
Chapter 4 67
Practical Sextant Usage 67
Taking a Sight – Step-by-Step Guide 67
Correct Handling and Positioning 71
Ensuring Accuracy in Sextant Readings 74
Reducing and Correcting Sightings 78
Index Error, Dip, and Refraction Corrections 79
Calculations for Accurate Results 80
Common Mistakes and Troubleshooting 81
Identifying and Avoiding Errors 83
Troubleshooting Techniques for Inaccuracies 87
Chapter 5 91

How to use a sextant for beginners

Advanced Celestial Navigation Techniques 91
  Noon Sights and Latitude Determination 91
    Using Noon Sight Method 92
    Latitude Calculations and Accuracy 93
  Time Sights and Latitude Determination 95
    Determining Longitude Using Time Sights 95
    Integrating Timekeeping 96
  Precision Navigation 97
    Averaging Sights for Precision 98
    Using Advanced Tools for Greater Accuracy 100
Chapter 6 102
Navigating with a Sextant 102
  Plotting Celestial Observations 102
    Transferring Sights to Nautical Charts 103
    Dead Reckoning and Celestial Navigation 105
  Real-World Applications 106
    Case Studies and Practical Examples 109
    Using Sextant Navigation in Diverse Navigational Scenarios 111
Chapter 7 114
The Future of Celestial Navigation 114
  Sextant Navigation in the Digital Age 114
    The Role of Sextants in the Era of GPS and Advanced Technology 117
  Exploring Advanced Topics 119
    Celestial Navigation in Space Travel 122
    Cutting-Edge Developments in Celestial Navigation Research 125

Conclusion 129

How to use a sextant for beginners

Introduction

In the quiet coastal town of Mariner's Cove, nestled between the gentle lapping waves of the sea and the vast expanse of the night sky, lived a curious young soul named Alex. From a very young age, Alex was entranced by the mysteries of the stars and the art of navigating the world's oceans. As the sun dipped below the horizon each evening, casting a tapestry of constellations across the heavens, Alex's fascination only grew.

One fateful night, while stargazing on the beach, Alex met an old sea captain named Captain Morgan. With a glint of wisdom in his eyes, Captain Morgan revealed the ancient secrets of celestial navigation, where mariners of old once guided their ships across the endless seas using nothing more than the stars, a sextant, and an unyielding spirit of adventure.

Inspired by this encounter, Alex embarked on a journey of discovery, pouring over ancient texts, practicing with a sextant under the vast night sky, and learning the delicate art of interpreting the language of the stars. As the days turned into weeks and the weeks into months, Alex's knowledge grew, and the stars above began to reveal their hidden patterns.

What You Will Learn

In this book, "How to Use a Sextant for Beginners," we invite you to embark on a similar adventure. Whether you're a novice sailor yearning to navigate the high seas with confidence, an adventurous spirit eager to explore the world's mysteries, or a seasoned explorer seeking to reconnect with ancient maritime traditions, this book is your guiding star.

Here, you will uncover the fundamental principles of celestial navigation, demystify the intricate workings of the sextant, and learn how to find your position on Earth using the same techniques that guided mariners for centuries. Through clear explanations, step-by-step guides, and practical examples, you will gain the knowledge and skills to harness the power of the stars for your own journeys.

Who Needs This Book

This book is for the dreamer who gazes at the night sky and wonders about the far-off lands it conceals. It's for the sailor setting sail into the unknown, equipped not only with modern technology but also with the wisdom of ancient seafarers. It's for the adventurer who seeks the thrill of exploration, guided by the constellations above.

Whether you're planning a grand voyage across the oceans, a weekend sailing trip, or simply wish to unravel the mysteries of the night sky from your backyard, "How to Use a Sextant for Beginners" is your compass. Through these pages, you will not only learn the art of celestial navigation but also embark on a transformative journey, connecting with the age-old wisdom of those who sailed before you.

So, dear reader, let the stars be your guide and this book be your map. Together, we will navigate the vastness of the cosmos and the depths of the sea, unveiling the secrets that have captivated explorers and dreamers for centuries. Welcome to a world where the sky meets the sea, and adventure knows no bounds.

Welcome and Introduction to Celestial Navigation

Celestial navigation is a method of navigating by observing the positions of celestial bodies, such as the Sun, Moon, stars, and planets. This ancient technique has been used by sailors for centuries to determine their location and direction when out at sea, far from recognizable landmarks. Here's a basic introduction to celestial navigation:

Key Celestial Bodies:

1. **Sun:** The most commonly used celestial body for navigation. Its position changes predictably throughout the day.

2. **Moon:** Also widely used, though its position changes more rapidly than the Sun.
3. **Stars:** Certain bright stars are used as reference points. They appear fixed relative to each other.
4. **Planets:** Like stars, planets have predictable movements across the sky and can be used for navigation.

Navigational Tools:

1. **Sextant:** A precision instrument used to measure the angle between a celestial body and the horizon.
2. **Nautical Almanac:** A publication providing data about the positions of celestial bodies at specific times.
3. **Chronometer:** A highly accurate clock used to determine Greenwich Mean Time (GMT).
4. **Star Finder or Planisphere:** A map of the night sky, allowing sailors to identify stars and their positions at specific times.

Basic Concepts:

1. **Latitude:** Celestial navigation helps determine latitude (north-south position) accurately.
2. **Longitude:** Determining longitude (east-west position) requires accurate timekeeping, as the Earth rotates 15 degrees per hour.

Steps in Celestial Navigation:

1. **Take Sight:** Use a sextant to measure the angle between the celestial body and the horizon.
2. **Calculate Intercept:** Subtract the measured angle from 90 degrees to get the angle from the celestial body to the zenith (directly overhead point).
3. **Consult Nautical Almanac:** Find the declination (celestial latitude) and Greenwich Hour Angle (GHA) of the celestial body for the observed time.
4. **Calculate Latitude:** Subtract or add the intercept angle from the body's declination to find the ship's latitude.
5. **Calculate Longitude:** Compare the observed GHA with the Local Hour

Angle (LHA) to find the time difference. One hour of time difference equals 15 degrees of longitude.

Challenges:

- **Weather:** Cloudy skies obstruct celestial bodies.
- **Accuracy:** Precise measurements and calculations are crucial.
- **Experience:** Skill and practice are required to master celestial navigation.

Celestial navigation, while traditional, is still taught and used today, especially in contexts where GPS systems might fail or be unavailable, making it an important skill for sailors and navigators to learn.

Importance of Learning Sextant Navigation in the Modern Age

Learning sextant navigation in the modern age holds significance for several reasons, despite the prevalence of advanced GPS technology. Here are some reasons why mastering sextant navigation remains important:

1. **Redundancy and Backup:**

    - **GPS Reliability:** GPS systems can fail due to technical issues, signal jamming, or solar flares. Sextant navigation provides a reliable backup method, crucial for sailors on long journeys or in remote areas.

2. **Emergency Situations:**

    - **Lost Signal:** In emergencies, such as a malfunctioning GPS device, knowledge of sextant navigation can help determine a vessel's approximate position, aiding search and rescue efforts.

3. **Historical Significance:**

    - **Preserving Tradition:** Sextant navigation is a centuries-old technique, and learning it helps preserve maritime traditions and cultural heritage.

4. Educational and Skill Development:

- **Nautical Education:** Learning sextant navigation enhances understanding of astronomy, mathematics, and geography, fostering a well-rounded education for maritime enthusiasts and professionals.
- **Problem-Solving Skills:** Sextant navigation requires complex calculations, honing problem-solving abilities and critical thinking.

5. Deepening Understanding:

- **Comprehensive Knowledge:** Understanding both traditional and modern navigation methods provides a more comprehensive grasp of navigation principles, making sailors more versatile and knowledgeable.

6. Navigating Challenging Environments:

- **Polar Regions:** Near the poles, GPS signals can be unreliable. Navigators in polar regions may need to rely on celestial navigation techniques.

- **Space Exploration:** Astronauts and spacecraft use celestial navigation principles when navigating in space, making it a fundamental skill for future space exploration.

7. Cultural Exploration:

- **Celestial Navigation in Cultures:** Knowledge of celestial navigation enhances cultural exploration, allowing individuals to understand the historical navigation methods of different cultures around the world.

8. Professional Mariner Requirements:

- **Certification and Regulations:** Some professional maritime certifications still require proficiency in celestial navigation as a part of the curriculum, ensuring that mariners maintain traditional skills alongside modern technologies.

9. Appreciation of Nature:

- **Connection with Nature:** Sextant navigation fosters a deep connection with the natural world, encouraging navigators to observe the skies and appreciate the beauty of celestial bodies.

In summary, while GPS technology has revolutionized navigation, the art of sextant navigation remains relevant, offering backup solutions, preserving heritage, enhancing education, and providing a deeper understanding of the world and the cosmos. Learning this traditional skill equips navigators with a holistic perspective on their craft, making them more versatile and resourceful professionals.

Chapter 1
The Basics of Celestial Navigation

Understanding Celestial Navigation

In the vast expanse of the open ocean, where the boundaries between sea and sky blur into an endless canvas of mystery, celestial navigation emerges as the ancient art that connects seafarers to the very fabric of the cosmos. At its core, celestial navigation is a dance of precision and intuition, a symbiotic relationship between the mariner and the stars. It's a practice as old as time itself, where the celestial bodies above – the radiant Sun, the enigmatic Moon, and the distant stars – become guiding lights, shaping the course of ships across uncharted waters.

Imagine a sailor, standing on the deck of a ship beneath a tapestry of stars. Armed with a sextant, this navigator measures the angle between the horizon and the North Star, Polaris, its unwavering gleam providing a beacon amidst the darkness. With swift calculations and a touch of celestial magic, the sailor determines the ship's latitude, unlocking the secrets of their position on the Earth's surface. It's a method that defies the constraints of technology, relying instead on the keen eyes of the observer and the timeless movements of heavenly bodies. Celestial navigation is more than just a skill; it's a connection to the cosmos, a tradition that whispers stories of ancient mariners and their unwavering spirit of exploration. In the following chapters, we will unravel the mysteries of celestial navigation, delving into its techniques, its history, and the profound sense of wonder it evokes in those who venture to master it.

Historical Significance and Evolution

In the annals of human exploration, celestial navigation stands as a testament to humanity's ingenuity, patience, and insatiable curiosity about the world beyond the horizon. Dating back thousands of years, this celestial dance of seafaring captivated the hearts and minds of ancient civilizations. From the Phoenicians navigating the Mediterranean to the Polynesian voyagers crossing the vast Pacific, celestial navigation was the compass guiding these intrepid souls through uncharted waters. It was the celestial bodies above that provided the earliest mariners with their only reliable means of orientation, shaping the course of their journeys and influencing the tides of history.

As the centuries rolled by, celestial navigation evolved, adapting to the changing face of technology while retaining its intrinsic value. During the Age of Exploration, when brave sailors set forth to discover new worlds, celestial navigation became indispensable. It was a skill guarded like a precious secret, passed down from generation to generation, ensuring that the knowledge of the stars remained alive. With the advent of the sextant in the 18th century, the accuracy of celestial calculations soared, enabling mariners to pinpoint their location with unprecedented precision.

In the modern era, with the rise of satellites and advanced electronics, one might assume celestial navigation has faded into obsolescence. Yet, its legacy endures. The methods and principles that guided explorers of old continue to captivate navigators, scholars, and adventurers alike. The lore of ancient star maps and the wisdom of bygone astronomers remain relevant, reminding us of our roots and the profound connection between humanity and the cosmos. In this chapter, we will embark on a journey through time, tracing the historical significance of celestial navigation and exploring how it has adapted, persevered, and left an indelible mark on the tapestry of human exploration.

Relevance in Modern Navigation

In an era dominated by satellites and cutting-edge GPS technology, the question arises: does celestial navigation still hold relevance in the modern world? The answer is a resounding yes. While GPS has undoubtedly revolutionized navigation, celestial techniques remain indispensable for several compelling reasons.

1. **Redundancy in Navigation:** Despite the reliability of GPS, redundancy is vital in navigation. Aboard ships, aircraft, or even spacecraft, having a backup method ensures safety in case of GPS failure due to technical glitches, jamming, or other unforeseen circumstances. Celestial navigation, with its independence from electronic systems,

provides a reliable fallback, essential for both civilian and military applications.

2. **Challenging Environments:** GPS signals can be compromised in certain environments, such as polar regions or densely populated urban areas with signal interference. In these challenging settings, where GPS accuracy falters, celestial navigation stands strong. Explorers, aviators, and mariners operating in these regions rely on the timeless guidance of the stars to plot their courses accurately.

3. **Space Exploration:** Beyond Earth's atmosphere, where GPS signals fade into the cosmic silence, celestial navigation takes center stage. Spacecraft traveling vast interstellar distances and rovers exploring other planets use celestial principles to determine their positions and orientations. The same techniques that guided ancient mariners across oceans now guide humanity's exploration of the cosmos.

4. **Educational and Cultural Significance:** Celestial navigation remains a cornerstone of maritime education, instilling a deep understanding of astronomical concepts,

mathematics, and geography. Additionally, it preserves cultural heritage, ensuring that the wisdom of ancient navigators is not lost to the march of progress. Learning these methods cultivates a profound connection between generations, nurturing respect for tradition and the vastness of the universe.

5. **Human Element and Skill Development:** Beyond its practical applications, celestial navigation enhances the human element of navigation. It sharpens problem-solving skills, fosters keen observation, and instills confidence in mariners. Mastering this art form transcends the practical; it becomes a testament to human intellect and adaptability, reminding us that the wonders of the universe are within our grasp.

In the modern age, where technology often eclipses tradition, celestial navigation stands resilient. Its continued relevance is a testament to its enduring importance, not merely as a backup system but as a bridge between our terrestrial existence and the boundless celestial realm. As we delve further into this chapter, we will explore the contemporary applications of celestial navigation, delving into its use in diverse fields and understanding the unique advantages it offers in our fast-paced, technology-driven world.

Introduction to Sextants

Anatomy and Components

At the heart of celestial navigation lies the quintessential tool of the trade: the sextant. An elegant instrument, the sextant bridges the vast expanse between Earth and sky, allowing navigators to capture the very essence of celestial bodies. Its design is both simple and intricate, embodying centuries of nautical wisdom and scientific precision.

1. The Sextant's Anatomy:

At first glance, a sextant appears as a metallic frame adorned with various scales, mirrors, and a telescope. Its primary purpose is to measure the angular distance between celestial objects and the horizon or between two celestial objects. Let's dissect its anatomy:

- **Frame:** The backbone of the sextant, usually made of brass, provides stability and houses the essential components.
- **Index Arm:** Extending from the frame, the index arm holds the index mirror and moves along the arc or scale.
- **Horizon Mirror:** Positioned at the front of the sextant, this mirror reflects the image of the celestial body and the horizon, allowing simultaneous observation.
- **Index Mirror:** Located at the rear of the index arm, this mirror reflects the image of the celestial object into the telescope.
- **Telescope:** Mounted on the frame, the telescope enables precise sighting of celestial bodies. It often has a magnifying lens for accurate readings.
- **Shade Glasses:** Sextants come with various shades of glasses, used to protect the observer's eyes from the Sun's intense glare during daytime observations.

2. Components and Working Principle:

The sextant operates on the fundamental principle of measuring angles. When a navigator sights a celestial body through the telescope, they align it with the horizon. The sextant's index arm is then adjusted until the reflected image of the celestial body aligns with the horizon in the horizon mirror. The angle is read directly from the sextant's scale.

- **Arc or Scale:** The graduated arc along which the index arm moves. It is marked in degrees, minutes, and sometimes seconds, allowing precise measurement of angles.
- **Vernier Scale:** A fine-scale on the sextant that enhances accuracy by allowing readings between the main scale divisions.
- **Micrometer Drum:** Some sextants feature a micrometer drum connected to the index arm. This provides even finer adjustments, enabling highly accurate measurements.
- **Clamping Mechanism:** The sextant has a clamping system to secure the index arm once the desired angle is achieved, ensuring the reading remains stable.

Understanding the intricacies of the sextant's anatomy and components is fundamental to mastering celestial navigation. In the chapters to come, we will explore how this remarkable instrument, guided by skilled hands and keen eyes, transforms celestial observations into precise navigational data, guiding sailors across the endless ocean expanses with unerring accuracy.

Types of Sextants and Their Uses

Sextants, diverse in design and functionality, have evolved over centuries to meet various navigational needs. Each type caters to specific environments and purposes, enhancing the versatility of celestial navigation. Let's explore the prominent types of sextants and their distinct uses:

1. **Davis Quadrant:**

   - **Design:** The Davis Quadrant, an early precursor to the sextant, features a 90-degree arc with a sighting vane.
   - **Use:** Primarily used for measuring the altitude of celestial bodies above the horizon, the Davis Quadrant was popular during the Age of Exploration.

2. **Quadrant Sextant:**

   - **Design:** Similar to the Davis Quadrant, the Quadrant Sextant has a 90-degree arc but includes mirrors for more accurate readings.
   - **Use:** Historically used for lunar distance observations, determining a ship's longitude based on the Moon's position relative to stars or planets.

3. **Octant:**

   - **Design:** The octant has a 45-degree arc, allowing measurements up to 90 degrees by reflecting the image twice.
   - **Use:** Widely used in the 18th century for celestial navigation, especially in

the calculation of latitude and longitude.

4. **Sextant:**

- **Design:** The modern sextant features a 60-degree arc, making direct measurements of angles easier.
- **Use:** Standard tool for celestial navigation on ships, aircraft, and even space missions. It is versatile, capable of measuring the altitude of celestial bodies and angular distances between them.

5. **Quintant:**

- **Design:** An extended version of the sextant, offering a 72-degree arc for even more precise measurements.
- **Use:** Rarely used today, quintants were historically employed for highly accurate celestial observations, especially in scientific research and astronomy.

6. **Marine Sextant:**

    - **Design:** A robust and weather-resistant sextant designed for maritime use, often made of brass or bronze.
    - **Use:** Standard navigational tool for sailors, enabling precise measurement of celestial angles at sea, essential for determining a ship's position and course.

7. **Bubble Sextant:**

    - **Design:** A variation of the marine sextant with a built-in bubble level for ensuring the instrument is perfectly horizontal.
    - **Use:** Commonly used in aircraft and small boats where stability is a challenge. The bubble helps maintain accuracy during measurements.

Each type of sextant has its unique advantages, making them suitable for specific navigational scenarios. While the marine sextant remains the go-to, choice for most maritime applications, understanding the diverse types equips navigators with the knowledge to choose the most appropriate instrument for their specific needs. In the following chapters, we will delve deeper into the practical applications of these sextants, exploring their usage in various celestial navigation techniques and real-world scenarios.

Fundamental Principles

Angle Measurement and Angular Distance

At the heart of celestial navigation lies the fundamental principle of measuring angles. In the vast expanse of the sky, mariners and astronomers alike rely on precise angle measurements to determine the positions of celestial bodies and, consequently, their own locations on Earth. Understanding the concepts of angle measurement and angular distance is pivotal for mastering the art of celestial navigation.

1. **Angle Measurement:**

- **Degrees, Minutes, and Seconds:** Angles in celestial navigation are typically measured in degrees (°), minutes ('), and seconds ("). There are 60 minutes in a degree and 60 seconds in a minute, allowing for highly accurate measurements.
- **Using a Sextant:** A sextant measures the angle between two objects, usually a celestial body and the horizon. The sextant's scale, often graduated in degrees and minutes, allows navigators to measure these angles with precision.

2. **Angular Distance:**

- **Definition:** Angular distance refers to the separation between two celestial bodies or a celestial body and a specific point in the sky, measured in degrees, minutes, or seconds.
- **Using Angular Distance:** Navigators use angular distance to determine their position or time. For example, the distance between the Moon and a specific star can be used to calculate time, while the angle between two stars can help establish latitude.

3. **Parallax and Correction:**

    - **Parallax:** Celestial objects are so distant that their positions appear fixed in the sky. However, when observed from different points on Earth's surface, there is a slight shift due to parallax. Navigators must correct measurements to account for this effect.
    - **Corrections:** Various corrections, such as dip and refraction, account for the observer's height above sea level and atmospheric effects. These corrections ensure accurate angle measurements, vital for precise navigation.

4. **Altitude and Zenith Distance:**

    - **Altitude:** The altitude of a celestial body is its angle above the observer's horizon. A celestial body on the horizon has an altitude of 0°, while directly overhead, it has an altitude of 90°.
    - **Zenith Distance:** Zenith distance is the complement of altitude, representing the angle between a

celestial body and the observer's zenith (the point in the sky directly above the observer). Zenith distance + altitude = 90°.

5. **Converting Angular Measurements:**

- **Decimal Degrees:** Angular measurements can be converted into decimal degrees for mathematical calculations, providing a convenient way to work with angles in various formulas.
- **Trigonometric Functions:** Trigonometric functions like sine, cosine, and tangent are used to calculate angles and distances in celestial navigation, forming the basis for many navigational computations.

Mastering the principles of angle measurement and angular distance equips navigators with the foundation needed to accurately interpret sextant readings, enabling them to unlock the secrets of celestial navigation. As we move forward, we will explore practical applications of these principles, guiding navigators through real-world scenarios and celestial calculations.

Relationship between Earth, Celestial Bodies, and Observer

In the intricate tapestry of celestial navigation, understanding the dynamic relationships among Earth, celestial bodies, and the observer is paramount. These relationships form the basis of celestial calculations, allowing navigators to pinpoint their locations on Earth's vast oceans or in the depths of space. Let's delve into the profound interconnections that define this celestial dance.

1. Earth's Rotation and the Celestial Sphere:

- **Apparent Motion:** Due to Earth's rotation, celestial bodies appear to move across the sky. The celestial sphere is an imaginary sphere surrounding Earth, upon which all celestial objects are considered to lie. It simplifies the complex three-dimensional motions of celestial bodies into a two-dimensional

framework for observation and calculation.
- **Diurnal Motion:** Celestial bodies rise in the east, reach their highest point (culmination) in the sky, and set in the west due to Earth's rotation. This diurnal motion varies with latitude and observer's position.

2. **Celestial Coordinates:**

- **Right Ascension and Declination:** Similar to Earth's longitude and latitude, celestial bodies are located on the celestial sphere using right ascension (measured in hours, minutes, and seconds) and declination (measured in degrees, minutes, and seconds). Right ascension is measured eastward along the celestial equator from the vernal equinox point.
- **Ecliptic Coordinates:** The ecliptic is the apparent path of the Sun across the celestial sphere. Celestial bodies are often described in terms of their ecliptic longitude and latitude, defining their positions relative to the Sun's apparent path.

3. Observer's Position and Horizon System:

- **Zenith and Nadir:** The zenith is the point directly above the observer, while the nadir is the point directly below. Understanding the positions of celestial bodies in relation to the zenith and nadir is crucial for determining their altitudes and azimuths.

- **Altitude and Azimuth:** Altitude is the angle between a celestial body and the observer's horizon, measured vertically. Azimuth is the angle between the celestial body and the observer's north, measured clockwise. These parameters help locate celestial bodies in the observer's local sky.

4. Solar and Sidereal Day:

- **Solar Day:** A solar day is the time interval between two successive solar noons when the Sun is at its highest point in the sky. It is approximately 24 hours long and determines our everyday concept of a day.

- **Sidereal Day:** A sidereal day is the time it takes for a celestial body to return to the same position in the sky, approximately 23 hours, 56 minutes, and 4 seconds. Sidereal time is used in celestial navigation for accurate star observations.

5. **Parallax and Atmospheric Effects:**

    - **Parallax:** The apparent shift in the position of a celestial body due to the observer's change in position on Earth. Parallax corrections are essential in celestial navigation, ensuring accurate measurements.
    - **Atmospheric Effects:** Earth's atmosphere refracts light, affecting the apparent positions of celestial bodies near the horizon. Corrections for atmospheric refraction are necessary for precise navigation, especially during low-altitude observations.

Understanding these intricate relationships allows navigators to interpret celestial observations effectively. In the chapters ahead, we will explore how these relationships are applied practically, guiding navigators through the complexities of celestial calculations and helping them determine their positions with unparalleled accuracy.

Chapter 2

Nautical Almanacs and Essential Tools

Navigational Almanacs

In the realm of celestial navigation, the Nautical Almanac stands as an indispensable guide, an astronomer's alchemy of numbers and charts that unlocks the secrets of the celestial sphere. This sacred tome, eagerly awaited by navigators each year, is a compendium of astronomical data meticulously calculated, offering a roadmap to the positions of celestial bodies with unparalleled accuracy.

1. **Astronomical Ephemerides:**

    - **Celestial Positions:** The Nautical Almanac provides the calculated positions of celestial bodies for each day of the year, expressed in terms of right ascension and declination. These positions serve as the foundation for celestial calculations, enabling navigators to determine their own positions on Earth.
    - **Timekeeping:** The almanac includes Greenwich Mean Time (GMT) and its corresponding Universal Time (UT1), essential for celestial calculations that require precise timing.

2. **Rise, Culmination, and Set Times:**

    - **Predicting Events:** For navigators, knowing when celestial bodies rise above the horizon, reach their highest point (culmination), and set below the horizon is crucial. The almanac provides these times, aiding in the planning of celestial observations.

- **Visibility and Observability:** Understanding the times of celestial events helps navigators assess the visibility and observability of specific stars, planets, or the Moon during their navigational journeys.

3. **Altitude and Azimuth Tables:**

- **Altitude and Azimuth Values:** Navigators use the almanac's altitude and azimuth tables to find the altitude (angle above the horizon) and azimuth (angle measured clockwise from the north) of celestial bodies at specific times. These values are pivotal for sight reductions, a process used to determine a ship's position based on celestial observations.
- **Interpolation:** The almanac provides data for specific intervals (usually hourly), requiring navigators to interpolate values for times between these intervals. This interpolation skill is essential for accurate calculations.

4. **Additional Celestial Phenomena:**

- **Eclipses:** The Nautical Almanac predicts solar and lunar eclipses, detailing the times, magnitudes, and geographic regions where these phenomena are visible. This information aids navigators in understanding unusual variations in celestial observations caused by eclipses.
- **Planet and Moon Data:** The positions of planets and the Moon are crucial for celestial navigation. The almanac provides their coordinates, enabling navigators to incorporate these celestial bodies into their calculations.

The Nautical Almanac, with its wealth of astronomical data, serves as the cornerstone of celestial navigation. Navigators pore over its pages, extracting vital information that guides them across the open seas. Armed with the almanac and other essential tools, mariners embark on a celestial odyssey, navigating the world's waters by the timeless wisdom of the stars. In the subsequent chapters, we will explore other pivotal tools and techniques, unveiling the artistry of celestial navigation in its entirety.

Structure and Content

Within the crisp pages of the Nautical Almanac lies a meticulously organized wealth of celestial data, a celestial navigator's treasure trove. Understanding the structure and content of this venerable tome is akin to deciphering the language of the stars. Let's unravel the intricacies of its structure and delve into the celestial secrets it holds.

1. **Annual Sections:**

   - **Rising and Setting Times:** The almanac provides rising and setting times for the Sun and Moon, crucial for determining daylight and nighttime hours. This information aids in planning celestial observations and navigating based on visible celestial bodies.
   - **Moon Phases:** Lunar phases, including new moon, first quarter, full moon, and last quarter, are essential for understanding the Moon's visibility and brightness during different parts of the month.

2. **Monthly Pages:**

- **Daily Celestial Data:** Each month is detailed on separate pages, offering daily data for celestial bodies such as the Sun, Moon, planets, and selected stars. This includes their right ascension, declination, Greenwich Mean Time (GMT), and other pertinent information.
- **Aries Ephemeris:** The Aries ephemeris, a reference to the vernal equinox, provides celestial positions at 0 hours GMT. Navigators use this data as a baseline for celestial calculations, adjusting for specific times during the day.

3. **Additional Sections:**

- **Star Charts:** Star charts or diagrams illustrate the positions of stars and constellations in the night sky. Navigators use these charts to identify and observe specific stars, aiding in celestial sightings and calculations.
- **Correction Tables:** Correction tables for factors like parallax, refraction, and semidiameter are included. These

tables are vital for adjusting celestial observations made near the horizon, ensuring accurate readings.

- **Explanatory Notes:** The almanac often includes explanatory notes, providing clarifications on calculations, tables, and astronomical phenomena. These notes offer valuable insights into the nuances of celestial navigation.

4. **Special Events:**

- **Eclipses:** Detailed information about solar and lunar eclipses, including dates, times, magnitudes, and geographic regions of visibility, are presented. Navigators can anticipate and account for the effects of eclipses on celestial observations.
- **Planet Data:** Positions of planets such as Venus, Mars, Jupiter, and Saturn are provided, allowing navigators to incorporate these celestial bodies into their calculations for advanced celestial navigation techniques.

The meticulous structure and comprehensive content of the Nautical Almanac empower celestial navigators with the knowledge needed to chart their course across the open seas. Its pages, adorned with celestial coordinates and astronomical events, are a testament to humanity's enduring fascination with the cosmos. In the subsequent chapters, we will explore how mariners harness this information, transforming raw data into navigational wisdom.

How to Read and Interpret

The Nautical Almanac, with its labyrinth of numbers and charts, holds the key to celestial navigation. To the untrained eye, its pages might seem cryptic, but to a seasoned navigator, they unfold a celestial ballet. Let's embark on the journey of decoding this astronomical manuscript, learning the art of reading and interpreting its data.

1. **Understanding Celestial Coordinates:**

    - **Right Ascension and Declination:** Right ascension (RA) and declination

(Dec) are celestial coordinates akin to Earth's longitude and latitude. RA is measured in hours, minutes, and seconds, while Dec is measured in degrees, minutes, and seconds. These coordinates pinpoint the positions of celestial bodies on the celestial sphere.

2. **Deciphering Rising and Setting Times:**

- **Sun and Moon Rising and Setting Times:** The almanac provides the GMT times when the Sun and Moon rise above the horizon and set below it. These times are crucial for determining daylight hours and night visibility, aiding in celestial observations.

3. **Utilizing Correction Tables:**

- **Parallax and Refraction Corrections:** Near the horizon, celestial objects appear slightly higher due to atmospheric effects. Correction tables in the almanac account for parallax and refraction, allowing navigators to adjust observed altitudes accurately.

4. **Applying Interpolation Techniques:**

    - **Interpolating Values:** The almanac provides data at specific intervals, often hourly. Navigators must interpolate values for times between these intervals. This skill is vital for obtaining accurate celestial data for a specific moment.

5. **Reading Star Charts:**

    - **Identifying Constellations and Stars:** Star charts in the almanac depict constellations and stars visible in the night sky. Navigators use these charts to identify celestial bodies, aiding in sightings and calculations.

6. **Analyzing Ephemerides Data:**

    - **Daily Ephemerides:** The almanac presents daily data for celestial bodies, including their right ascension, declination, and GMT. Navigators use this data for various calculations, such as determining their latitude and longitude using celestial sights.

7. **Utilizing Lunar Distances:**

- **Lunar Distance Tables:** Lunar distances involve measuring the angular distance between the Moon and another celestial body, usually a star or planet. The almanac provides tables for these distances, allowing navigators to calculate their Greenwich Hour Angle (GHA) and local mean time.

8. **Incorporating Planetary Data:**

- **Planet Positions:** The almanac provides positions for planets such as Venus, Mars, Jupiter, and Saturn. Navigators incorporate these positions into their calculations, enabling advanced celestial navigation techniques.

Decoding the Nautical Almanac's data requires patience, practice, and a deep understanding of celestial navigation principles. As we progress through the following chapters, we will explore practical scenarios, demonstrating how to apply this knowledge to real-world celestial navigation challenges.

Additional Tools for Celestial Navigation

Beyond the sextant and the Nautical Almanac, celestial navigators employ a range of supplementary tools to enhance accuracy, efficiency, and safety during their voyages across the open seas. These tools, both traditional and modern, complement the navigator's skillset and provide valuable assistance in celestial calculations. Let's explore some of these additional tools that navigate the mariner through the celestial realm.

1. **Marine Chronometer:**

    - **Precision Timekeeping:** A marine chronometer is a highly accurate clock designed to keep precise time aboard a moving ship. Accurate time is crucial for celestial navigation, especially when calculating longitude using celestial sights.

2. **Sight Reduction Tables:**

    - **Reduction to Almanac Values:** Sight reduction tables, often provided in compact books, simplify the process of reducing sextant observations to values found in the Nautical Almanac. These tables streamline complex calculations, saving time and ensuring accuracy.

3. **Azimuth Tables:**

- **Determining Azimuth:** Azimuth tables assist in determining the azimuth of celestial bodies, which is the angle measured clockwise from the north. Knowing azimuth is vital for establishing the direction of a celestial body relative to the observer, aiding in navigation.

4. **Almanac Correction Tables:**

- **Correcting Almanac Values:** Almanac correction tables account for various corrections required when using data from the Nautical Almanac. Corrections for factors such as refraction, parallax, and semidiameter are essential for precise celestial calculations.

5. Star and Planet Identifiers:

- **Star Finders:** Star finders are handheld devices with rotating discs, helping navigators identify stars and constellations in the night sky. These aids enhance the navigator's ability to locate specific celestial bodies for observations.
- **Planetarium Software:** Modern navigators often use planetarium software, available on computers and mobile devices, to simulate the night sky. These applications provide real-time celestial positions, aiding in identifying and planning observations.

6. Astronomical Almanacs:

- **Astronomical and Air Almanacs:** In addition to the Nautical Almanac, celestial navigators may refer to astronomical almanacs that offer detailed data on celestial events, planetary positions, and lunar phases. Air almanacs provide data specifically for aviation purposes.

7. **GPS Backup Systems:**

- **Satellite Communicators:** Satellite communicators with GPS capabilities serve as reliable backup systems. In case of sextant or electronic GPS failure, these devices provide accurate position information, ensuring navigators stay on course.

8. **Handheld GPS Devices:**

- **Emergency Navigation:** Handheld GPS devices, designed for outdoor and marine use, serve as emergency backup tools. While not traditionally used for celestial navigation, they can provide latitude and longitude information in emergencies.

By harnessing the power of these additional tools, celestial navigators equip themselves with comprehensive resources, enhancing their ability to navigate accurately and confidently. In the chapters to come, we will explore how these tools synergize with the navigator's expertise, guiding them through complex celestial calculations and real-time navigation challenges.

Chapter 3
Celestial Bodies and Their Navigation

The Sun: Your Primary Celestial Object

The Sun, our primary celestial guide, is essential for celestial navigation. Its high visibility allows for daytime observations. Using the sextant, mariners measure the Sun's angle above the horizon to determine their latitude. By observing the Sun's altitude at solar noon and applying corrections, navigators obtain accurate readings, aiding in position fixes and maintaining course on the open seas.

Taking Sights on the Sun

Taking sights on the Sun is a fundamental celestial navigation technique. Using a sextant, navigators measure the Sun's altitude above the horizon during clear daytime conditions. By carefully aligning the sextant, noting the exact time of the observation, and applying necessary corrections for factors like parallax and refraction, sailors can determine their latitude. This technique provides a reliable method for fixing a ship's position, ensuring safe and accurate navigation under the Sun's guidance.

Corrections and Calculations

In celestial navigation, precise calculations are essential. Navigators apply corrections to observed celestial data, accounting for factors like parallax, refraction, and vessel's height of eye. These corrections refine the measurements, ensuring accuracy. With corrected data in hand, mariners then perform intricate calculations, employing trigonometry and interpolation. These calculations yield crucial information: the celestial body's true position, aiding in determining the vessel's latitude and longitude accurately. Mastery of corrections and calculations forms the backbone of celestial navigation, guiding seafarers confidently across the vast ocean expanse.

Navigating by the Moon, Planets, and Stars

Celestial navigation extends beyond the Sun. Navigators utilize the Moon, planets, and stars as celestial landmarks. By measuring their altitudes with a sextant, mariners determine their positions. Lunar distances between the Moon and other celestial bodies offer a unique method for finding Greenwich time. Planets like Venus and stars such as Polaris are valuable reference points. Skilled celestial navigators decipher these celestial puzzles, using the ever-moving celestial bodies to chart precise courses across the open waters.

Methods for Taking Sights on Various Celestial Bodies

Celestial navigation encompasses a variety of methods for observing different celestial bodies, each with its unique techniques and applications. Navigators' adept in these methods can pinpoint their positions with remarkable accuracy. Let's explore these techniques in detail:

1. **Sights on the Sun:**

    - **Daytime Sights:** Using a sextant, observers measure the Sun's altitude above the horizon during daylight hours. The sight should be taken when the Sun is neither too high nor too low, ensuring accurate readings.
    - **Noon Sight:** Solar noon, when the Sun is at its highest point, provides the most straightforward observation. By measuring the Sun's altitude at this moment, navigators can calculate their latitude directly.

2. **Sights on the Moon:**

- **Lunar Observations:** Measuring the Moon's altitude during both day and night yields valuable information. Daytime lunar sights provide a backup to solar observations, while nighttime lunar sights are used in conjunction with stars for longitude calculations.
- **Lunar Distances:** Navigators measure the angular distance between the Moon and other celestial bodies, a method historically crucial for determining Greenwich time and consequently, longitude.

3. **Sights on Planets:**

    - **Planetary Observations:** Planets such as Venus, Mars, Jupiter, and Saturn are bright and easily identifiable. Their sights are used similarly to lunar observations, providing data for position fixes, especially when other celestial bodies are not visible.
    - **Planetary Eclipses:** Observing a planet as it enters or exits the Earth's shadow (a planetary eclipse) provides a unique opportunity for precise

timing, aiding in longitude calculations.

4. **Sights on Stars:**

   - **Stellar Observations:** Stars serve as reliable reference points, especially during nighttime. Navigators measure the altitudes of specific stars using a sextant, enabling latitude calculations.
   - **Circumpolar Stars:** Stars that never set below the horizon, like Polaris in the Northern Hemisphere, provide continuous reference points. Observations of circumpolar stars aid in determining latitude.

5. **Combining Observations:**

   - **Multiple Sights:** Navigators often take sights on multiple celestial bodies within a short timeframe. By combining these observations, they can cross-check their calculations, enhancing accuracy and confidence in their navigational fix.
   - **Meridian Passages:** Observing celestial bodies as they cross the observer's meridian (an imaginary

line from north to south) provides accurate timing, crucial for longitude calculations.

Mastering these methods requires a keen eye, precision in sextant usage, and a deep understanding of celestial mechanics. Skilled celestial navigators expertly choose the appropriate celestial bodies based on visibility and time, employing these methods to navigate confidently across the world's oceans, guided by the timeless lights of the cosmos.

Overcoming Challenges and Pitfalls

Celestial navigation, while elegant and precise, is not without its challenges. Mariners face various pitfalls that demand expertise and resilience. Understanding and overcoming these challenges is essential for successful celestial navigation:

1. **Weather Conditions:**

    - **Overcast Skies:** Thick cloud cover obscures celestial bodies, rendering

sightings impossible. Navigators must patiently await clear skies or rely on alternative navigation methods until celestial observations become feasible.
- **Hazy Atmosphere:** Atmospheric haze can distort the apparent positions of stars and planets, leading to inaccurate readings. Experienced navigators account for these distortions in their calculations.

2. **Equipment Issues:**

    - **Sextant Errors:** Calibration errors or instrument damage can introduce inaccuracies. Regular maintenance and careful calibration are necessary to ensure the sextant's precision.
    - **Timekeeping Devices:** Malfunctioning clocks or chronometers can result in incorrect time, affecting longitude calculations. Navigators must carry backup timepieces and periodically check their accuracy against reliable sources.

3. **Observer Errors:**

- **Parallax Errors:** Incorrect positioning of the eye in relation to the sextant's mirrors can lead to parallax errors, especially during rough seas. Vigilance and proper technique are essential to minimize these errors.
- **Interpolation Mistakes:** Human error in interpolating values from tables can lead to significant calculation errors. Navigators must double-check their calculations, ensuring accuracy in all interpolations.

4. **Navigational Challenges:**

- **Determining Longitude:** Longitude calculations, especially without accurate timekeeping, pose a considerable challenge. Navigators need to rely on a combination of celestial observations, dead reckoning, and, if available, radio signals for accurate longitude fixes.
- **Navigating Near Land:** Celestial navigation close to shore demands careful consideration of land-based obstacles and navigational aids.

Mariners must integrate visual cues with celestial observations for precise coastal navigation.

5. Continuous Training and Adaptation:

- **Skill Maintenance:** Celestial navigation is a perishable skill. Mariners must continuously practice and update their knowledge to maintain proficiency, especially in the age of electronic navigation systems.
- **Adapting to Modern Tools:** While celestial navigation remains invaluable, mariners must adapt to modern navigation technologies. Integrating celestial observations with electronic navigation systems enhances navigational redundancy and safety.

Navigators overcome these challenges through a combination of experience, training, and adaptability. By honing their skills, remaining vigilant, and embracing the synergy between traditional celestial methods and contemporary technologies, mariners confidently traverse the seas, undeterred by the complexities of celestial navigation.

Special Cases and Techniques

In the intricate art of celestial navigation, special cases and techniques offer navigators nuanced methods for precise positioning and course correction. These advanced approaches, born from centuries of seafaring wisdom, empower mariners to navigate challenging scenarios. Let's delve into these special cases and techniques:

1. **Compass Deviation Corrections:**

   - **Magnetic Deviation:** Earth's magnetic field affects compass readings, leading to deviation errors. Navigators apply specific corrections to adjust for these errors, ensuring accurate bearings for celestial observations.

2. **Time Sight Method:**

   - **Time Sight Calculations:** Navigators can determine their longitude using a single celestial body, a sextant, and a highly accurate timepiece. By comparing the observed altitude of the celestial body with its calculated altitude at the time of observation, mariners calculate their Greenwich Hour Angle (GHA), facilitating longitude calculations.

3. **Sumner Lines:**

- **Sumner Line Plotting:** When multiple celestial bodies are observed simultaneously, Sumner lines help navigators pinpoint their vessel's position where these lines intersect. This method is invaluable for fixing a position with high precision.

4. **Dip Short and Depression of the Horizon:**

- **Dip Short Corrections:** In low light or rough seas, the horizon might appear higher than it actually is, leading to incorrect altitude readings. Navigators apply dip short corrections to account for this discrepancy.
- **Depression of the Horizon:** In cold weather or at high altitudes, the

horizon may appear lower than normal. Corrections for the depression of the horizon compensate for this effect, ensuring accurate altitude measurements.

5. **Advanced Lunar Distance Techniques:**

- **Time Azimuth Method:** Utilizing lunar distances and accurate timekeeping, navigators calculate their longitude using the time azimuth method. This technique provides an alternative approach for longitudinal fixes, especially in lunar distance observations.

6. **Using Artificial Horizon:**

- **Artificial Horizon Devices:** Mariners can use artificial horizons, like a liquid-filled pan, to create a stable, reflective surface for celestial observations. This technique is valuable on ships with limited stability or in challenging weather conditions.

7. **Emergency Celestial Navigation:**

- **Backup Techniques:** In emergency situations where sextants or precise timepieces are unavailable, mariners can use improvised sighting tools, like a quadrant made from basic materials. These rudimentary tools enable rough celestial observations, providing essential navigational information.

Mastery of these special cases and techniques elevates celestial navigation from a skill to an art form. Experienced navigators draw upon this deep knowledge, adapting their methods to diverse situations, ensuring safe passage even in the most challenging maritime conditions.

Twilight Navigation

Twilight, that magical period between sunset and darkness, and its counterpart before sunrise, holds unique significance in celestial navigation. Navigators' adept in twilight observations utilize the residual light in the sky to continue their celestial fixes when traditional nighttime stars are yet to emerge or have faded away. During the evening twilight, celestial objects like planets, bright stars, and the Moon often remain visible, providing reference points for sextant readings. These twilight sights enable mariners to prolong their navigational activities, enhancing their ability to determine their positions accurately.

Twilight navigation requires a keen understanding of celestial bodies' behaviour during these transitional periods. During the evening twilight, navigators can still measure the altitudes of celestial objects before they disappear below the horizon. Similarly, in the morning twilight, celestial objects become visible before the sky fully brightens, allowing for early observations. Twilight observations demand meticulous planning, as the changing light conditions affect the sextant's accuracy. Mariners must be aware of the specific twilight phases, such as civil twilight (when the Sun is just below the horizon and the sky is still illuminated) and nautical twilight (when the Sun is between 6 and 12 degrees below the horizon), to optimize their observations.

Twilight navigation serves as a bridge between daylight and nighttime celestial fixes, providing navigators with extended opportunities for position fixes. Skillful mariners capitalize on this unique period, combining their knowledge of twilight phenomena with the art of celestial navigation. By honing their ability to read the skies during these subtle transitions, navigators harness the fleeting moments of twilight to refine their positions and ensure the uninterrupted progress of their vessels on the vast expanse of the open sea.

Stellar Navigation and Fixing Positions at Night

Navigating by the stars, known as stellar navigation, unveils a celestial tapestry that guides mariners during the night. Under the veil of darkness, specific constellations and stars become steadfast companions, aiding sailors in determining their positions on the open sea. By measuring the altitudes of these stellar bodies using a sextant, mariners can calculate their latitude. The North Star, Polaris, holds particular significance in the

Northern Hemisphere, as it remains almost stationary and aligned with the Earth's axis, serving as a reliable reference point for determining true north. In the Southern Hemisphere, navigators often rely on the Southern Cross and other prominent constellations for orientation. Stellar navigation demands a deep understanding of star charts and celestial mechanics, allowing seafarers to identify stars, determine their altitudes, and subsequently deduce their latitude with precision.

When the night sky is adorned with an array of stars, skilled navigators extend their celestial fix to calculate longitude. By measuring the angle between a known star or planet and the Moon or another celestial body, mariners can ascertain their Greenwich Hour Angle (GHA). This information, combined with the time of observation, enables the calculation of the vessel's longitude. This method, known as lunar distance, offers a powerful tool for nighttime celestial navigation. With meticulous observation and accurate timekeeping, mariners can triangulate their positions, ensuring a safe and accurate course even under the vast canopy of the night sky.

Chapter 4
Practical Sextant Usage

Taking a Sight – Step-by-Step Guide

Navigators, both seasoned and novice, embark on a celestial odyssey armed with their sextants, seeking to capture the essence of the celestial bodies and translate them into precise navigational data. Here, in a step-by-step guide, lies the art of taking a celestial sight using a sextant, demystified and made accessible:

1. **Prepare Your Sextant:**

    - **Check Alignment:** Ensure the index arm and the horizon glass are properly aligned. Any misalignment could result in inaccurate readings.

- **Adjust the Index Error:** Zero the sextant by adjusting the index arm until the horizon glass reflects the visible horizon perfectly.
- **Set the Time:** Note the exact time of the sight. Precision in timekeeping is vital for accurate celestial calculations.

2. **Select the Celestial Body:**

- **Choose Wisely:** Select a celestial body such as the Sun, Moon, star, or planet. Consider its altitude – celestial bodies higher in the sky are preferable for accurate readings.
- **Identify the Body:** Use star charts, almanacs, or planetarium software to identify the chosen celestial body.

3. **Take the Sight:**

- **Steady the Sextant:** Hold the sextant firmly against your eye. Use the index finger to move the index arm gently.
- **Align with the Horizon:** While looking through the sextant, bring the celestial body down to the visible

How to use a sextant for beginners

horizon. Keep both in view simultaneously.
- **Stop at the Horizon:** The exact moment the celestial body touches the horizon is your reading point. Record the angle indicated on the sextant.

4. **Apply Corrections:**

    - **Parallax Correction:** Correct for parallax by estimating the observer's height of eye and applying the appropriate correction, ensuring the observation is relative to the sea horizon.
    - **Dip Correction:** Correct for dip, the apparent rise of the horizon when viewed from a height. Apply the dip value corresponding to your observer's height of eye.
    - **Refraction Correction:** Account for atmospheric refraction, which affects the apparent position of celestial bodies near the horizon. Refer to tables in the almanac for the correction value.

5. **Calculate Altitude:**

- **Subtract Corrections:** Subtract the dip, parallax, and refraction corrections from the observed sextant altitude.
- **Final Altitude:** The corrected value represents the celestial body's true altitude above the horizon at the time of observation.

6. Record and Use:

- **Note Observational Data:** Record the observed altitude, the celestial body, the time of the observation, and all applied corrections.
- **Use for Navigation:** Utilize the corrected altitude in celestial navigation calculations to determine your position on Earth's vast expanse.

With these steps, the celestial realm becomes accessible to the navigator. Each sight taken is a mark of precision, a testament to the artistry of celestial navigation. Armed with the knowledge of sextant usage, mariners traverse the oceans, guided by the timeless dance of the stars, the Moon, and the Sun.

How to use a sextant for beginners

Correct Handling and Positioning

Mastering the sextant goes beyond understanding its parts; it's about finesse in handling and precision in positioning. Here's a guide to ensure correct handling and positioning, crucial for accurate celestial observations:

1. **Firm but Gentle Grip:**

    - **Hold Steadily:** Hold the sextant firmly but without excessive force. A steady grip ensures stability during observations, especially in the rolling and pitching of a ship.
    - **Avoid Jerky Movements:** Smooth, deliberate movements prevent jarring, which can misalign the sextant and lead to erroneous readings.

2. **Eye Placement:**

    - **Proper Eye Alignment:** Place your eye correctly at the sight vane. Your eye should align naturally without straining, ensuring accurate readings.
    - **Avoid Parallax:** Adjust the index mirror to eliminate parallax. Parallax

occurs when the observer's eye is not in line with the index mirror, causing apparent shifts in celestial body positions.

3. **Positioning during Observation:**

- **Stable Platform:** Rest your elbows on a stable surface, like a bulkhead or a railing. This minimizes body movement, crucial for maintaining a steady aim while sighting.
- **Maintain Horizontality:** Keep the sextant horizontal during the observation. Tilt the sextant gently until the celestial body touches the horizon. A stable horizon and a level sextant are essential for accurate readings.

4. **Observing Body's Center:**

- **Center the Body:** Always align the observed celestial body with its reflected image in the index mirror. The body should be precisely centered to avoid angle discrepancies.
- **Steady Adjustment:** Make adjustments smoothly. Jerky motions

might displace the celestial body, leading to incorrect altitude readings.

5. Protect from Light Pollution:

- **Shield from Light:** Shield the sextant from artificial lights, especially during twilight or nighttime observations. Even a faint light source can interfere with celestial sightings.

6. Regular Maintenance:

- **Clean and Calibrate:** Regularly clean the sextant's mirrors and lenses. Proper calibration ensures accurate angle measurements. Check for any signs of wear or damage and address them promptly.

7. Proper Storage:

- **Secure Storage:** Store the sextant in a sturdy case when not in use. Protect it from moisture, extreme temperatures, and physical impacts. Proper storage prolongs the sextant's lifespan and maintains its accuracy.

By adhering to these guidelines, mariners elevate the sextant from a mere instrument to a precise extension of their navigational acumen. With skillful handling and precise positioning, celestial observations transform from mere measurements to reliable data, guiding seafarers across the vast ocean expanse with unwavering accuracy.

Ensuring Accuracy in Sextant Readings

In the delicate dance of celestial navigation, accuracy in sextant readings is paramount. Here's a comprehensive guide to ensuring precision, elevating your celestial observations to an art of exactitude:

1. **Sextant Inspection:**

    - **Regular Checks:** Before each use, inspect the sextant for any signs of damage, corrosion, or misalignment. Ensure all parts move smoothly without resistance.
    - **Clean Optics:** Clean the sextant's mirrors and lenses meticulously to remove any smudges or particles,

guaranteeing clear, unobstructed views.

2. **Proper Calibration:**

   - **Index Error:** Accurately measure and adjust the index error to zero. A calibrated sextant ensures readings are aligned precisely with the celestial body's position.
   - **Collimation Check:** Verify that the mirrors are perfectly aligned (collimated). Misaligned mirrors can distort readings significantly.

3. **Practicing Consistent Technique:**

   - **Steady Grip:** Maintain a steady grip on the sextant, avoiding sudden movements that could misalign the instrument during readings.
   - **Consistent Eye Placement:** Ensure your eye is consistently positioned at the same point on the sextant's arc during observations. This consistency minimizes parallax errors.

4. **Minimizing Human Error:**

- **Attention to Detail:** Double-check all data entries, ensuring correct values for time, altitude, and corrections. Even a minor mistake can lead to significant navigational errors.
- **Patience in Measurements:** Exercise patience during observations, waiting for the celestial body to stabilize. Rushed readings often result in inaccuracies.

5. **Weather and Environmental Considerations:**

- **Stable Platform:** Seek stable platforms, especially on a moving vessel. Rest your elbows on a solid surface to minimize body sway, ensuring a stable sextant position.
- **Lighting Conditions:** Be mindful of lighting conditions, especially during twilight. Shield the sextant from artificial lights and allow your eyes to adjust to low-light environments.

6. **Cross-Verification and Redundancy:**

- **Multiple Observations:** Take multiple sights of the same celestial

body to cross-verify readings. Consistent readings enhance confidence in the observed data.
- **Use Redundant Systems:** Combine celestial navigation with other navigation methods, like GPS, for redundancy. In critical situations, cross-verification ensures the accuracy of your position.

7. **Continuous Training:**

- **Skill Enhancement:** Regularly practice celestial navigation to maintain and enhance your skills. Familiarity and proficiency are key to accurate readings.
- **Stay Updated:** Stay abreast of new techniques, tools, and corrections. Continuous learning ensures you apply the most accurate methods in your observations.

By adhering to these principles, navigators infuse their sextant readings with unwavering accuracy. Each reading becomes a testament to precision, guiding seafarers confidently across the globe's vast and unpredictable oceans.

Reducing and Correcting Sightings

After the sextant captures the celestial body's altitude, the navigator enters the realm of reduction and correction, transforming raw observations into accurate navigational data. First, meticulous corrections are applied, compensating for factors like parallax, refraction, and instrumental errors. These corrections refine the initial reading, ensuring it represents the true altitude of the celestial body above the horizon. Additionally, dip and index corrections are crucial, accounting for the observer's height and sextant index error, respectively, further enhancing accuracy.

Next, these corrected altitudes are reduced to obtain their corresponding declinations and Greenwich Hour Angles (GHAs) using data from the Nautical Almanac. This reduction process involves intricate calculations, often employing interpolation techniques to determine celestial body positions between tabulated values. Once these computations are complete, navigators possess a precise celestial fix, a point in the vast expanse of the ocean determined by the meticulous interplay of sextant, mathematics, and astronomical data. This navigational prowess ensures accurate course plotting and guides mariners safely on their voyages, even amidst the challenges of the open sea.

Index Error, Dip, and Refraction Corrections

In celestial navigation, three critical corrections—Index Error, Dip, and Refraction—fine-tune raw sextant observations. **Index Error Correction** accounts for any misalignment in the sextant's index mirror, ensuring precise altitude measurements. **Dip Correction** adjusts for the apparent rise of the horizon when viewed from a height, a crucial consideration especially on a moving vessel. Finally, **Refraction Correction** compensates for the bending of light as it passes through the Earth's atmosphere, affecting celestial bodies' apparent positions near the horizon. These corrections are meticulous, often involving trigonometric calculations, and are pivotal in transforming observed altitudes into accurate celestial data, laying the foundation for precise navigational fixes on the open sea.

Calculations for Accurate Results

In the realm of celestial navigation, precise calculations serve as the linchpin between sextant readings and accurate positional fixes. Navigators engage in intricate computations, employing trigonometry and interpolation techniques to reduce observed altitudes, calculate declinations, and determine Greenwich Hour Angles (GHAs). The celestial sphere's complex dance is deciphered through meticulous mathematics, ensuring that corrections for factors like parallax, refraction, and instrumental errors are seamlessly integrated. Through these calculations, mariners transform celestial observations into reliable latitude and longitude coordinates, charting their courses across the vast oceans with unparalleled accuracy. Each calculation is a testament to the navigator's skill, blending the art of mathematics with the poetry of the stars, guiding ships confidently in the timeless tradition of celestial navigation.

Common Mistakes and Troubleshooting

Navigating the celestial realm is an art demanding precision, yet even the most seasoned mariners can encounter pitfalls. This chapter unveils the common mistakes that befall celestial navigators and offers troubleshooting insights:

1. **Parallax Errors:**

    - **Mistake:** Incorrect eye positioning leading to parallax errors, affecting altitude readings.
    - **Troubleshoot:** Ensure consistent eye placement and confirm the index mirror's alignment to eliminate parallax discrepancies.

2. **Instrumental Errors:**

    - **Mistake:** Misaligned mirrors or inaccurate sextant calibration causing erroneous observations.
    - **Troubleshoot:** Regularly calibrate the sextant, verify collimation, and promptly address any damage or misalignment.

How to use a sextant for beginners

3. **Calculation Inaccuracies:**

- **Mistake:** Errors in reduction, interpolation, or computation, leading to imprecise celestial fixes.
- **Troubleshoot:** Double-check calculations, use reliable references, and recalibrate instruments if discrepancies persist.

4. **Timekeeping Issues:**

- **Mistake:** Incorrect time entries affecting Greenwich Hour Angle (GHA) calculations.
- **Troubleshoot:** Rely on precise timepieces, cross-verify with radio signals, and synchronize with official time sources.

5. **Insufficient Environmental Considerations:**

- **Mistake:** Ignoring environmental factors like unstable platforms or inadequate lighting conditions.
- **Troubleshoot:** Seek stable platforms for observations, shield the sextant

from light pollution, and adapt to changing environmental conditions.

6. **Overreliance on Technology:**

- **Mistake:** Overconfidence in electronic aids, neglecting traditional methods.
- **Troubleshoot:** Balance modern technology with traditional celestial skills, ensuring proficiency in both realms for reliable navigation.

By recognizing these pitfalls and embracing troubleshooting strategies, navigators fortify their celestial expertise. Through continuous learning and attention to detail, mariners ensure the mastery of celestial navigation, confidently steering their ships under the timeless guidance of the stars.

Identifying and Avoiding Errors

In the intricate art of celestial navigation, identifying and sidestepping errors is as crucial as capturing accurate readings. This chapter delves into the nuanced world of error recognition and prevention:

1. **Vigilant Observation:**

    - **Identify Patterns:** Analyze past mistakes to identify recurring patterns. Address these consistently to prevent future errors.
    - **Continuous Vigilance:** Stay vigilant during observations, scrutinizing instrument readings and calculations for inconsistencies.

2. **Precision in Instrumental Use:**

    - **Regular Maintenance:** Ensure instruments are well-maintained, calibrated, and collimated to avoid instrumental errors.
    - **Master Instrumental Use:** Continuously train in sextant usage, focusing on consistent eye placement and steady grip to minimize parallax and sighting errors.

3. **Calculation Accuracy:**

    - **Methodical Checks:** Implement a systematic approach to calculations, double-checking each step to catch errors before they compound.
    - **Peer Review:** Encourage peer reviews or cross-verification of calculations to detect potential mistakes.

4. **Environmental Awareness:**

    - **Adapt to Conditions:** Adjust observation techniques based on changing environmental factors, such as lighting and stability, to prevent observational errors.
    - **Anticipate Challenges:** Foresee challenges like adverse weather and prepare contingency plans, ensuring navigation remains accurate under varied conditions.

5. **Data Cross-Verification:**

    - **Multiple Sightings:** Take multiple sightings of the same celestial body and cross-verify the results.

Consistent readings enhance confidence in the observed data.
- **Utilize Redundancy:** Integrate electronic navigation systems, like GPS, as backup, enhancing reliability through data redundancy.

6. **Continuous Training:**

    - **Skill Enhancement:** Regularly practice celestial navigation to maintain and enhance skills. Familiarity and proficiency are key to error-free observations.
    - **Stay Updated:** Stay abreast of new techniques, tools, and corrections. Continuous learning ensures application of the most accurate methods in observations.

By adhering to these strategies, navigators bolster their celestial acumen, ensuring that errors are swiftly identified and avoided. Each celestial fix becomes a testament to meticulous preparation, guiding mariners confidently through the seas, even in the face of celestial intricacies.

Troubleshooting Techniques for Inaccuracies

In the intricate world of celestial navigation, inaccuracies can arise from various sources. This chapter explores advanced troubleshooting techniques, equipping navigators with the skills to pinpoint and rectify inaccuracies:

1. **Error Analysis:**

    - **Systematic Review:** Conduct a systematic review of the entire observation process, including instrument use, calculations, and environmental conditions.
    - **Error Localization:** Identify the stage (observation, reduction, or calculation) where the error likely occurred to focus troubleshooting efforts.

2. **Instrumental Diagnostics:**

    - **Sextant Calibration:** Re-calibrate the sextant, paying attention to index error and collimation. Even subtle

misalignments can cause significant discrepancies.
- **Mirror Inspection:** Thoroughly inspect mirrors and lenses for any defects, ensuring they are clean and free of scratches.

3. **Data Cross-Verification:**

- **Multiple Observers:** Involve multiple observers to cross-verify observations. Discrepancies among observers can indicate errors.
- **Inter-Body Checks:** Cross-verify observations between different celestial bodies to catch inconsistencies. Consistent errors across multiple observations might suggest systematic issues.

4. **Environmental Factors:**

- **Lighting and Stability:** Pay attention to lighting conditions and stability during observations. Even minor changes can impact accuracy. Shield the sextant from light pollution.
- **Atmospheric Corrections:** Be aware of atmospheric conditions affecting

refraction. Utilize tables and apply corrections accordingly.

5. **Advanced Calculation Techniques:**

- **Advanced Interpolation:** Employ advanced interpolation techniques for precise calculations, especially for declinations and Greenwich Hour Angles (GHAs).
- **Iterative Methods:** Implement iterative methods for complex calculations, refining results through successive approximations.

*6. **Historical Data Comparison:**

- **Historical Records:** Compare current observations with historical data. Discrepancies might indicate subtle instrument wear or changes in environmental conditions over time.
- **Experienced Mentoring:** Seek guidance from experienced celestial navigators, comparing your observations with their records to gain insights into potential errors.

Through these advanced troubleshooting techniques, navigators refine their ability to detect and rectify inaccuracies. In the face of complexity, these strategies ensure that celestial navigation remains a reliable and precise art, guiding mariners with unwavering accuracy across the expansive seas.

Chapter 5
Advanced Celestial Navigation Techniques

Noon Sights and Latitude Determination

Noon sights represent a fundamental technique in celestial navigation. When the Sun is at its zenith or highest point in the sky, mariners can measure its altitude directly, providing a straightforward method to determine latitude. By capturing the Sun's altitude at local noon and comparing it with the noon altitude recorded in navigational almanacs for that day's date and geographical position, navigators can calculate their latitude precisely. This technique offers a rapid and reliable way to establish one's position without relying on complex calculations, making it invaluable for quick latitude fixes during sea voyages.

Using Noon Sight Method

The Noon Sight method is a straightforward and efficient technique in celestial navigation, enabling mariners to determine their latitude accurately with minimal calculations. At local noon, when the Sun reaches its highest point in the sky, navigators use a sextant to measure the Sun's altitude above the horizon. This observed altitude is then compared with the declination of the Sun at that particular moment, as listed in navigational almanacs. The difference between the observed altitude and the Sun's declination represents the angle between the observer's position and the celestial body. By knowing the angle and the approximate Earth's radius, navigators can directly calculate their latitude. This method is particularly useful in clear weather conditions, allowing navigators to obtain a latitude fix swiftly, providing a reliable reference point for further navigation.

The Noon Sight method's simplicity and speed make it a preferred choice, especially in emergency situations or when other celestial bodies might be obscured. Navigators can swiftly execute this technique, ensuring a quick assessment of their position without delving into extensive calculations. By mastering this method, mariners enhance their navigational proficiency, confidently sailing the seas by harnessing the Sun's timeless guidance.

Latitude Calculations and Accuracy

Calculating latitude is a fundamental aspect of celestial navigation, ensuring accurate positioning on Earth's vast waters. Using celestial bodies like the Sun, Moon, or bright stars, mariners measure their observed altitude above the horizon with a sextant. This observed altitude is then compared to the celestial body's declination, the angular distance north or south of the celestial equator, which is found in navigational almanacs for a specific date and time. The difference between the observed altitude and the celestial body's declination represents the zenith distance, the angle between the celestial body and the observer's zenith (the point directly above the observer). Subtracting the zenith distance from 90 degrees gives the observer's latitude. These calculations are crucial for accurate latitude determination and serve as the foundation for plotting a ship's position on nautical charts.

Accuracy in latitude calculations demands precision in both sextant readings and the use of declination values. Even minor errors in these measurements can result in significant navigational discrepancies. Mariners must diligently correct for factors like dip, refraction, and parallax, which can affect observed altitudes. By adhering to proper techniques and meticulous calculations, navigators ensure the utmost accuracy in determining their latitude, enhancing their confidence in the ship's position and ultimately contributing to the safety and success of their maritime journeys.

Benjamin L. Hedwig

Time Sights and Latitude Determination

Time sights involve measuring the altitude of a celestial body, such as the Sun or a star, at two different times, allowing navigators to calculate both the latitude and the vessel's east-west position (longitude) accurately. By observing the same celestial body at two different times and noting the elapsed time between sightings, mariners can use tables and calculations to determine their latitude based on the celestial body's declination at the observed times. Time sights provide a robust method for celestial navigation, offering navigators the ability to refine their position with increased accuracy, especially during extended voyages or when other navigation aids are limited.

Determining Longitude Using Time Sights

Determining longitude accurately is a pivotal challenge in celestial navigation. Time sights offer a strategic solution. By capturing the altitude of a celestial body, such as the Sun, at two distinct times and meticulously recording the time difference between these sightings, navigators can calculate the Greenwich Hour Angle (GHA) of the celestial body. Comparing this GHA with the corresponding value from navigational almanacs provides the time difference between the observer's location and the Prime Meridian at Greenwich, England. Since the Earth rotates 15 degrees per hour, every 15-degree difference in GHA corresponds to a one-hour time difference, allowing mariners to deduce their longitude precisely. Time sights, when executed meticulously, enable navigators to unravel the mystery of longitude, paving the way for accurate course plotting and safe seafaring across vast oceans.

Integrating Timekeeping

In celestial navigation, accurate timekeeping is akin to possessing the key to a cryptic celestial code. Every celestial body's position is intricately linked to time, making precise time measurements paramount. Modern marine chronometers, designed for maritime use, ensure accurate timekeeping on ships. Integrating these chronometers with celestial observations is pivotal.

Observing celestial bodies at specific times and meticulously noting these times synchronizes with the chronometer's readings. By comparing the observed celestial angles with the corresponding values from navigational almanacs and adjusting for the time difference between the chronometer and the celestial observations, navigators can deduce their longitude accurately. This harmonious integration of celestial observations and precise timekeeping transforms the art of celestial navigation into a method of unparalleled accuracy, enabling mariners to chart their courses with confidence across the vast and unpredictable oceans.

Precision Navigation

Precision navigation in the modern era is a testament to the fusion of cutting-edge technology and traditional techniques. Advanced satellite-based Global Navigation Satellite Systems (GNSS) like GPS, GLONASS, and Galileo have revolutionized maritime navigation. These systems provide real-time positioning data with remarkable accuracy, enabling vessels to pinpoint their positions to within a few meters. Integrated with inertial navigation systems and electronic chart displays, ships can navigate intricate waterways and avoid hazards with unprecedented precision.

Yet, even in this high-tech landscape, the wisdom of traditional navigation methods endures. Celestial navigation, once the sole means of determining position at sea, is now a revered art. Mariners, equipped with sextants and almanacs, continue to hone their celestial skills, ensuring their ability to navigate even if satellite systems fail or in remote regions where signals might be weak. This harmonious blend of satellite-based systems and ancient celestial techniques epitomizes precision navigation in the modern age, safeguarding ships and their crews with redundant layers of navigational expertise.

Averaging Sights for Precision

Navigators often employ the technique of averaging sights to enhance the precision of their celestial fixes. By taking multiple sightings of the same celestial body over a span of time, mariners can mitigate the impact of small observational errors and random fluctuations, ensuring a more accurate position fix. Averaging sights involves carefully calculating the mean of these observations, effectively reducing the margin of error. This method is particularly valuable when celestial bodies are near the horizon, where their positions can be affected by atmospheric conditions and other environmental factors.

Averaging sights demands meticulous record-keeping, precise time measurements, and consistent observation techniques. By amalgamating multiple readings and computing their average, navigators enhance the reliability of their celestial fixes. This meticulous approach adds a layer of accuracy to their navigational data, contributing to safer voyages and more confident maritime journeys.

Using Advanced Tools for Greater Accuracy

In the modern era, navigators benefit from a plethora of advanced tools designed to enhance accuracy and precision. Electronic chart systems (ECS) and Electronic Navigational Charts (ENCs) provide real-time vessel positioning, detailed maps, and information about navigational hazards. Differential GPS (DGPS) and Real-Time Kinematic (RTK) systems offer centimeter-level accuracy, particularly valuable for precise coastal navigation and docking manoeuvres.

Additionally, inertial navigation systems, gyrocompasses, and accelerometers provide continuous data on a vessel's motion, aiding in course stabilization and accurate positioning. Advanced weather forecasting tools and oceanographic data systems allow mariners to anticipate and navigate through challenging weather conditions with greater confidence. Moreover, radar and sonar technologies ensure accurate detection of nearby vessels and underwater obstacles, enhancing collision avoidance capabilities.

Integrating these advanced tools with traditional navigation methods like celestial navigation and dead reckoning creates a comprehensive and redundant navigation system. This fusion of cutting-edge technology and time-honoured techniques ensures unparalleled accuracy, enabling mariners to navigate safely and confidently through the world's oceans, even in the most demanding conditions.

Chapter 6
Navigating with a Sextant

Plotting Celestial Observations

Navigating with a sextant involves transforming observed celestial data into tangible positions on nautical charts. After obtaining precise sextant readings, mariners meticulously plot these observations on the chart. Each celestial observation, converted into a line of position (LOP), represents a circle on the chart due to the Earth's rotation. Where these circles intersect signifies the vessel's potential position. By taking multiple LOPs from different celestial bodies and plotting them simultaneously, navigators refine their position further, pinpointing their location with enhanced accuracy.

Plotting celestial observations demands attention to detail and proficiency in chartwork. Mariners must factor in corrections for dip, refraction, and parallax while marking the LOPs. The intersection of these lines demands precision, often necessitating the use of specialized navigational tools like parallel rulers and dividers. As each observation is translated onto the chart, the vessel's position becomes an intricate tapestry woven from the artistry of celestial navigation. This process, blending meticulous observation with skilled chart plotting, exemplifies the essence of celestial navigation, guiding mariners confidently across the vast expanse of the seas.

Transferring Sights to Nautical Charts

Transferring sights from a sextant to nautical charts is a pivotal step in celestial navigation, where precision and meticulous attention to detail is paramount. After taking celestial observations and calculating the resulting lines of position (LOPs), mariners must accurately place these LOPs on their nautical charts to determine their vessel's position. This process involves several key steps:

1. **Identifying Celestial Bodies:** Mark the celestial bodies observed and note the exact times of observation. Identify each LOP with the respective celestial body, ensuring a clear record for plotting.
2. **Correction Application:** Apply corrections for factors like dip, refraction, and parallax to the observed altitudes, ensuring that the LOPs represent the true celestial body positions at the time of observation.
3. **Plotting LOPs:** Using a parallel ruler and dividers, carefully plot each LOP on the nautical chart. Position the LOP by the celestial body's observed altitude and time, ensuring the line is perpendicular to the azimuth at that time.
4. **Repeat for Multiple Observations:** For enhanced accuracy, repeat this process for each celestial body observed, plotting multiple LOPs on the chart.

5. **Intersection of LOPs:** The point where these LOPs intersect on the chart represents the vessel's potential position at the time of observation. The more LOPs plotted, the more accurately the vessel's position can be determined, refining the fix.

Transferring sights to nautical charts is both a science and an art, where mariners skilfully blend their technical knowledge with precision chartwork. This process is the gateway to navigating with precision and confidence, allowing ships to safely traverse the world's oceans by harnessing the guidance of the celestial realm.

Dead Reckoning and Celestial Navigation

The integration of dead reckoning (DR) and celestial navigation represents a harmonious blend of traditional and celestial techniques, enhancing navigational accuracy and reliability, especially on long ocean passages. Dead reckoning involves estimating a vessel's position based on its previously known position, course, speed, and time, factoring in the effects of current and wind. However, over time, DR positions can accumulate errors due to unpredictable factors.

Celestial navigation acts as a celestial reset, providing an accurate fix periodically. By combining celestial observations with the last known DR position, mariners can recalibrate their estimated position, significantly reducing cumulative errors. This integration ensures a continuous feedback loop between the vessel's predicted position (DR) and the actual celestial fix, allowing for timely corrections and precise course adjustments.

The integration process requires meticulous record-keeping, including regular celestial observations, accurate timekeeping, and consistent dead reckoning calculations. By marrying the calculated DR position with the celestial fix, mariners gain a more accurate understanding of their vessel's location, enabling them to navigate with confidence, even during extended periods between celestial sightings. This integration of time-honoured DR techniques with the celestial realm exemplifies the art and science of navigation, ensuring ships' safe passage across the world's oceans.

Real-World Applications

In the contemporary maritime landscape, celestial navigation continues to hold immense relevance and practicality. One of its primary applications is in **Ocean Crossings and Long-Distance Voyages**, where GPS signals might weaken or face interruptions. Navigators on long sea passages often rely on celestial fixes to cross vast expanses of open ocean accurately, ensuring the ship's precise positioning.

Emergency Navigation also underscores celestial navigation's importance. In the event of electronic navigation system failures due to technical issues or cyber threats, mariners can fall back on celestial techniques. Ships facing critical situations, such as loss of power or navigational equipment, can employ sextants and almanacs to obtain celestial fixes, guiding them to the nearest safe harbour.

Moreover, celestial navigation is pivotal in **Maritime Education and Training**. Nautical institutions across the globe incorporate celestial navigation into their curricula. Aspiring mariners learn this ancient art alongside modern techniques, fostering a deep understanding of the principles of navigation and ensuring they can navigate effectively in any circumstance.

Additionally, celestial navigation finds applications in **Astronomy and Scientific Research**. Scientists studying Earth's position, movement, and rotation utilize similar principles to those in celestial navigation, deepening our understanding of celestial mechanics and Earth's place in the universe.

Beyond the maritime realm, celestial navigation has even found its way into **Outdoor Adventure and Exploration**. Enthusiasts, from sailors on small vessels to hikers and wilderness explorers, often learn basic celestial techniques for orientation and wayfinding in remote environments, enhancing their survival skills.

In each of these real-world scenarios, celestial navigation stands as a testament to human ingenuity, offering a reliable and time-tested method for precise navigation, ensuring the safety and success of ventures across both sea and land.

Case Studies and Practical Examples

Case Study 1: The Vendée Globe Solo Sail Race in the Vendée Globe, a solo around-the-world sail race, skippers navigate the globe entirely on their own. During this grueling race, sailors often encounter adverse conditions, making electronic systems vulnerable. Celestial navigation becomes a vital skill. Skippers employ sextants to obtain accurate fixes, ensuring they stay on course, especially in areas with limited GPS reception.

Case Study 2: Polynesian Wayfinding Tradition The ancient Polynesians were master navigators who used celestial cues to explore and settle the vast Pacific Ocean.

Using stars, wind patterns, and the behaviour of ocean waves and wildlife, they could determine their position accurately. This indigenous knowledge, passed down through generations, demonstrates the precision achievable through celestial navigation without modern instruments.

Practical Example: Open Ocean Rescue Operation In a search and rescue mission in the open ocean, where a distressed vessel's electronic systems fail, coast guards can employ celestial navigation techniques. By taking sun sights during the day and star sights during the night, rescuers can calculate the vessel's approximate position. This information guides search efforts, ensuring they focus on the correct area, ultimately saving lives.

Practical Example: Remote Island Expedition During scientific expeditions to remote islands, where GPS signals might be unreliable or unavailable, researchers often use celestial navigation to establish the island's exact location. By taking multiple celestial sights and averaging the results, scientists can precisely determine the island's coordinates. This accurate data is crucial for ecological studies and conservation efforts.

These case studies and practical examples highlight the versatility and importance of celestial navigation in various contexts. From solo sailors circumnavigating the globe to indigenous traditions and critical rescue operations, celestial navigation continues to prove its value in both routine and challenging situations, showcasing its timeless relevance in the modern world.

Using Sextant Navigation in Diverse Navigational Scenarios

Scenario 1: Transoceanic Yacht Racing In transoceanic yacht races like the Rolex Fastnet Race, where yachts traverse vast distances across open seas, sailors often face electronic navigation system failures due to extreme conditions. Sextant navigation becomes essential for determining precise positions, ensuring the yachts stay on course, even amidst the challenging waters of the Atlantic.

Scenario 2: Remote Island Surveys Scientific expeditions to remote islands require accurate geographic data for research and conservation efforts. When GPS signals are unreliable due to the islands' isolation, surveyors use sextants to establish the islands' positions. This traditional method ensures precise mapping, aiding scientific studies and environmental preservation initiatives.

Scenario 3: Antarctic Exploration In the harsh and unpredictable environment of Antarctica, where electronic equipment is susceptible to extreme cold, polar explorers utilize sextants to navigate. By observing celestial bodies, even in the continuous daylight of polar summers, explorers can maintain accurate positioning, enabling safe exploration of this remote and challenging terrain.

Scenario 4: Backup Navigation on Commercial Ships Commercial vessels, despite their advanced navigation systems, often have sextants on board as backup tools. In case of GPS malfunctions due to signal jamming or cyber threats, mariners can resort to celestial navigation. This redundancy ensures that, even in emergency situations, ships can maintain their routes and avoid potential hazards.

Scenario 5: Historic Vessel Replicas Replica ships, such as those used in historical reenactments or maritime museums, often rely solely on traditional navigation methods, including sextant navigation. Navigators on these vessels use sextants and celestial observations to recreate historical voyages, immersing participants and visitors in the seafaring traditions of the past.

In these diverse navigational scenarios, sextant navigation proves its versatility and reliability. From competitive yacht racing to scientific expeditions and historic recreations, mariners continue to trust this centuries-old technique, ensuring accurate positioning and safe passage in various maritime endeavours.

Chapter 7
The Future of Celestial Navigation

Sextant Navigation in the Digital Age

In the digital age, where advanced technologies dominate maritime navigation, the future of celestial navigation, particularly sextant usage, remains both relevant and promising. Sextant navigation, far from being antiquated, is evolving in innovative ways, complementing digital tools and addressing emerging challenges:

1. **Hybrid Navigation Systems:** Maritime navigation is witnessing the emergence of hybrid systems, where traditional sextant

navigation acts as a backup to digital tools. Integrating sextant fixes with electronic data enhances redundancy, ensuring ships have multiple layers of navigation, crucial for safety and reliability.

2. **Education and Heritage Preservation:** While electronic systems dominate modern training, celestial navigation, including sextant use, is becoming an integral part of maritime education. Aspiring mariners are learning traditional methods, preserving this invaluable heritage. Educational initiatives ensure that the knowledge of sextant navigation continues to be passed down to future generations.

3. **Space Exploration and Colonization:** As humanity ventures into space exploration and potential colonization of other celestial bodies, celestial navigation principles will find application beyond Earth. Sextant-like instruments may aid astronauts in deep space missions, where traditional GPS systems are impractical, making celestial observations essential for interplanetary navigation.

4. **Sextant Apps and Augmented Reality:** The advent of sextant apps and augmented reality technologies is rejuvenating celestial navigation. Mobile applications simulate sextant usage, allowing enthusiasts to practice celestial observations virtually. Augmented reality glasses might soon provide real-time guidance, overlaying celestial bodies' positions, further bridging the gap between tradition and technology.

5. **Environmental Sustainability:** Sextant navigation promotes environmental sustainability. By reducing reliance on continuous electronic navigation, mariners can minimize their vessels' energy consumption and carbon footprint. The eco-conscious maritime industry may increasingly turn to celestial navigation, including sextant use, as part of sustainable navigation practices.

The future of sextant navigation lies at the intersection of tradition and innovation. By embracing digital enhancements and preserving the artistry of celestial navigation, mariners are shaping a future where the sextant remains an invaluable tool, ensuring safe and sustainable journeys on the seas and beyond.

The Role of Sextants in the Era of GPS and Advanced Technology

In the age of GPS and advanced technology, sextants continue to hold a significant and unique role in maritime and celestial navigation. Here are several key aspects defining their role:

1. **Redundancy and Reliability:** Sextants serve as vital backup tools. In scenarios where GPS signals might be jammed, spoofed, or disrupted, mariners can fall back on sextants. Their reliability ensures that ships can navigate accurately even in challenging situations, ensuring redundancy in navigational systems.

2. **Training and Education:** Sextants are invaluable for educational purposes. They provide a tangible connection to the history of navigation and teach fundamental principles. Aspiring navigators and maritime enthusiasts learn about the Earth's position in the cosmos and the intricacies of celestial

mechanics, fostering a deeper understanding of navigation beyond digital interfaces.

3. **Celestial Fix Verification:** Sextants play a crucial role in verifying celestial fixes obtained from electronic systems. Navigators often cross-verify GPS-derived positions with celestial fixes. If inconsistencies arise, sextant-based fixes act as a reliable means to confirm the vessel's true position, enhancing the overall accuracy of navigation.

4. **Emergency Navigation:** In emergency situations where electronic systems fail or face cyber threats, sextants are indispensable. Mariners can use celestial observations to calculate their position, ensuring a safe course to the nearest harbours. Sextants provide a lifeline, especially in critical situations, enabling ships to navigate without dependence on external signals.

5. **Long-Range Oceanic Navigation:** For vessels embarking on long-range oceanic voyages, especially those far from shore where GPS signals weaken, sextants offer continuous navigation capabilities.

Navigators can take regular celestial sights to maintain accurate positioning, ensuring the vessel's course remains on track throughout the journey.

6. Cultural and Historical Significance: Sextants carry cultural and historical significance. They symbolize the artistry of navigation and the resilience of traditional methods. Preserving this heritage is essential, as it fosters a sense of tradition and pride among mariners and navigators, emphasizing the importance of celestial navigation in maritime culture.

In summary, while GPS and advanced technology have revolutionized navigation, sextants remain essential tools, offering redundancy, education, emergency capabilities, and a connection to maritime heritage. Their enduring relevance underscores the continued importance of mastering the art and science of celestial navigation in the modern age.

Exploring Advanced Topics

Celestial navigation, an ancient art intertwined with the stars, continues to captivate navigators with its complexity and depth. In this chapter, we delve into advanced topics, expanding the horizons of celestial knowledge:

1. **Astronomical Phenomena and Navigation:** Explore intricate astronomical events, such as lunar distances, planetary conjunctions, and eclipses, and their applications in navigation. Navigators can harness these phenomena to refine their celestial fixes, adding layers of precision to their calculations.

2. **Advanced Star Sights and Planetary Navigation:** Delve into advanced techniques for observing stars and planets. Learn how mariners use specific stars, such as those in the Nautical Almanac, and planets like Venus, Mars, and Jupiter, for celestial fixes. Master the calculations involved in determining the vessel's position based on these celestial bodies.

3. **Timekeeping and Chronometers:** Explore the intricate world of chronometers and timekeeping. Understand the historical development of marine chronometers and their modern counterparts. Delve into the nuances of time measurement and its pivotal role in celestial navigation accuracy.

4. **Celestial Navigation in Aviation:** Extend celestial navigation into the realm of aviation. Discover how pilots use celestial observations, including the moon and stars, as navigational aids, especially during long-haul flights where GPS signals might weaken. Learn about the unique challenges and advantages of celestial navigation at high altitudes.

5. **Digital Celestial Navigation Tools:** Investigate cutting-edge digital tools designed for celestial navigation. Explore celestial navigation software, applications, and augmented reality solutions that aid mariners and aviators in their celestial endeavours. Understand how these tools integrate traditional methods with modern technology.

6. Celestial Navigation and Space Travel: Envision celestial navigation's role in future space missions. Explore the challenges and opportunities of navigating in deep space, where traditional methods intersect with astrodynamics and interplanetary travel. Contemplate the importance of celestial navigation in humanity's quest for interstellar exploration.

By delving into these advanced topics, navigators and enthusiasts alike can deepen their understanding of celestial navigation, unveiling the intricacies that lie beyond the basics. Mastery of these advanced concepts empowers mariners and aviators to navigate with unparalleled precision, bridging the ancient celestial realm with the cutting-edge technologies of the future.

Celestial Navigation in Space Travel

In the vast expanse of space, celestial navigation transcends its terrestrial origins, becoming an indispensable tool for interstellar exploration. Here, in the boundless cosmic arena, celestial navigation takes on a new dimension:

1. **Interplanetary Trajectory Planning:** Celestial navigation guides spacecraft between planets. By calculating trajectories based on celestial body positions, space agencies plot paths that optimize fuel efficiency, ensuring precise interplanetary travel. Celestial fixes act as interstellar signposts, guiding probes and rovers through the cosmic sea.

2. **Deep Space Navigation:** Beyond our solar system, celestial navigation becomes crucial for deep space probes. Voyaging into the unknown, these probes utilize stars, galaxies, and pulsars as fixed reference points. By triangulating their positions with these cosmic beacons, spacecraft navigate vast interstellar distances with remarkable accuracy.

3. **Stellar Parallax and Astrometry:** Celestial navigation incorporates stellar parallax—a phenomenon where stars appear to shift against the background due to Earth's orbit. Astrometric measurements of this parallax help astronomers map the

universe's vastness. In space travel, understanding stellar parallax aids in gauging distances to stars and galaxies, essential for navigation in uncharted cosmic territories.

4. **Pulsar-Based Navigation:** Pulsars, rapidly rotating neutron stars emitting regular beams of radiation, serve as celestial lighthouses in space. Spacecraft equipped with X-ray detectors use pulsar signals for navigation. By measuring the arrival times of pulsar pulses, spacecraft precisely determine their position and velocity, enabling navigation even in the depths of intergalactic space.

5. **Relativity and Celestial Navigation:** Einstein's theory of relativity impacts celestial navigation in space. General relativity predicts the bending of light around massive celestial bodies. Spacecraft trajectories near massive stars and black holes require precise adjustments to account for gravitational lensing, ensuring accurate navigation amidst intense gravitational fields.

6. **Exoplanet Exploration:** Celestial navigation aids exoplanet hunters in locating distant planetary systems. By studying the subtle dimming of starlight as exoplanets transit their host stars, astronomers determine exoplanet positions. This data informs future interstellar missions, guiding humanity's quest to explore habitable worlds beyond our solar system.

Celestial navigation in space travel is not merely a historical relic but a visionary tool guiding humanity toward the cosmic frontiers. In the boundless reaches of the universe, celestial navigation illuminates our path, enabling mankind's exploration of distant stars, galaxies, and the mysteries that lie beyond.

Cutting-Edge Developments in Celestial Navigation Research

In the realm of celestial navigation, ongoing research and technological advancements are reshaping the way we perceive and utilize this ancient art. Here are the latest cutting-edge developments in celestial navigation research:

1. **Quantum Celestial Navigation:** Quantum technologies are revolutionizing celestial navigation. Quantum sensors, leveraging principles of quantum mechanics, provide ultra-precise measurements of gravity and time. Integrating quantum sensors with celestial observations enhances the accuracy of fixes, paving the way for unprecedented precision in space and maritime navigation.

2. **Machine Learning and Celestial Patterns:** Machine learning algorithms are being applied to vast astronomical datasets. These algorithms analyze celestial patterns, predicting the positions of stars, planets, and other celestial bodies with remarkable accuracy. Machine learning models, trained on historical celestial data, enable real-time celestial navigation calculations, ensuring continuous and reliable fixes.

3. **Space-Based Celestial Navigation Systems:** Deploying dedicated space-based telescopes for celestial navigation is a burgeoning field. These telescopes,

positioned in Earth's orbit, provide unobstructed views of the celestial sphere. Coupled with advanced imaging technologies, they offer uninterrupted observations, enabling continuous fixes even in adverse atmospheric conditions, bolstering the reliability of celestial navigation.

4. **Integrated Sensor Fusion:** Research focuses on integrating celestial navigation with other sensors like accelerometers, magnetometers, and gyroscopes. Sensor fusion algorithms combine data from multiple sources, compensating for each sensor's limitations. This integrated approach enhances navigation systems' resilience, ensuring consistent and accurate positioning in various environments and scenarios.

5. **Celestial Navigation in Autonomous Systems:** Autonomous vehicles and drones are increasingly relying on celestial navigation. Miniaturized sensors and specialized algorithms allow these systems to perform celestial fixes autonomously. Celestial navigation provides an independent, global, and natural reference

frame, ensuring the precise positioning of autonomous platforms in both terrestrial and extraterrestrial environments.

6. **Quantum Communication for Celestial Data Transmission:** Quantum communication protocols are being explored for secure transmission of celestial data. Quantum key distribution ensures the integrity and confidentiality of celestial observations sent between spacecraft, ground stations, and navigation centers. This quantum secure communication infrastructure safeguards the integrity of celestial navigation data, crucial for mission-critical applications.

Incorporating these cutting-edge developments, celestial navigation research is on the brink of a transformative era. The fusion of quantum technologies, artificial intelligence, space-based observatories, integrated sensor systems, and secure communication protocols propels celestial navigation into the future, shaping a new paradigm where the ancient art of navigating by the stars meets the forefront of scientific innovation.

Benjamin L. Hedwig

Conclusion

Congratulations, dear reader, on completing this journey into the intricate world of celestial navigation with a sextant. Throughout this book, you've delved into the rich history, learned the essential techniques, and explored the practical applications of this age-old art form. By mastering the use of a sextant, you've acquired a skill that not only connects you with centuries of seafaring tradition but also equips you with the ability to navigate the vast expanses of our world with confidence and precision.

As you embark on your own celestial navigation adventures, remember that learning is a continuous voyage. Practice, patience, and a curious spirit will be your best companions. With each sighting of the sun, moon, or stars, you refine your understanding of the cosmos and your place within it. The art of sextant navigation is not merely a historical relic but a timeless skill that empowers you to navigate both the seas of the world and the limitless possibilities of your own potential.

We hope this book has been a guiding star on your celestial journey. Your newfound knowledge is a testament to your dedication and curiosity. As you venture forth, may your sextant always be steady, your sights always true, and your journeys always safe.

We Value Your Feedback

If this book has been a valuable resource in your pursuit of celestial navigation mastery, we kindly invite you to share your thoughts by leaving a review on Amazon. Your feedback not only helps us understand how this book has benefited you but also assists fellow readers in making informed choices. We appreciate your support and look forward to hearing about your experiences with "Sextant for Beginners."

Safe travels, clear skies, and happy navigating!

Warm regards,

Benjamin L. Hedwig

How to use a sextant for beginners

Benjamin L. Hedwig

Printed in Great Britain
by Amazon